Contents

PRANAV PANDYA

OVERCOMING ADVERSITIES

Inspiring Stories of

Resilience And Triumph

Inkfeathers Publishing
www.inkfeathers.com

Overcoming Adversities
by Pranav Pandya
Paperback Edition

First Published in 2023 by

Inkfeathers Publishing
Vivek Vihar, New Delhi 110095
www.inkfeathers.com

ISBN 978-81-960895-6-6

Author's Note

Adversity is an inevitable part of life, and it can take many forms: from the loss of a loved one to a serious illness, to financial struggles, to discrimination and injustice. At times, adversity can feel insurmountable, and we may wonder how we will ever be able to recover from the setbacks and challenges we face.

But as the stories in this book demonstrate, adversity can also be a catalyst for growth, resilience, and transformation. The individuals featured in these pages have all faced tremendous obstacles and setbacks, but they have also found within themselves the strength, determination, and resourcefulness to overcome them.

Their stories are a testament to the power of the human spirit to persevere and thrive in the face of adversity. They remind us that even in our darkest moments, we can summon the courage and resilience to move forward, find hope, and create a new future for ourselves.

It is my hope that the stories in this book will inspire and uplift you, and that they will serve as a reminder that no matter what challenges we may face in life, we always have the capacity to overcome them.

Thank you for embarking on this journey of inspiration and hope with us.

Best regards,

Pranav Pandya

Introduction

The Power of Resilience

Life is full of challenges and obstacles, and at times it can seem like the weight of the world is upon our shoulders. Whether it's a health issue, a financial setback, or a personal tragedy, adversity can strike at any moment and leave us feeling overwhelmed and defeated. However, it is in these moments that our true character is tested, and our ability to persevere and overcome becomes essential.

Resilience is the foundation of our ability to face adversity and come out stronger on the other side. It is what allows us to push through the pain, the disappointment, and the setbacks and to keep moving forward toward our goals and dreams. It is the fuel that keeps us going when everything else seems to be against us.

In this book, we will explore the inspiring stories of individuals who have faced incredible adversity and yet managed to triumph in the face of it all. From illness to injury, from financial ruin to personal loss, these individuals have overcome obstacles that would have broken most of us and have emerged stronger and more determined than ever.

Through their stories, we will learn about the power of resilience and how it can help us to overcome even the most daunting challenges. We will see that resilience is not something that is reserved for the lucky or the privileged but is something that anyone can develop and cultivate, no matter what their circumstances may be.

Step in on this journey of inspiration and discovery, as we explore the incredible power of resilience and the triumph of the human spirit.

Chapter One

From Tragedy to Triumph

Overcoming Loss and Grief

The human experience is one filled with both joy and pain. We all experience moments of happiness and moments of sorrow. However, some people face unimaginable loss and grief that can be difficult to overcome. Yet, these individuals find a way to rise above their circumstances and create a life filled with purpose and meaning.

In this chapter, we will explore the stories of those who have faced the devastating loss of a loved one, a career, or a dream, and have found the strength to move forward despite the pain.

Let's read the story of Mary Johnson, who forgave the man who murdered her only son and went on to create a foundation to bring together families of victims and offenders. We will also learn about the journey of author and speaker Joan Didion, who wrote "The Year of Magical Thinking" after the sudden death of her husband and daughter, and how she found hope in the midst of despair.

Through these stories and others, we will see how resilience can be a powerful tool in the face of loss and grief. We will learn how these individuals were able to find meaning in their pain and use it to create something positive for themselves and others.

While everyone's journey is unique, these stories remind us that it is possible to overcome even the most unimaginable circumstances.

Incredible resilience and forgiveness

The Story of Mary Johnson

Mary Johnson's story is one of incredible resilience and forgiveness. In 1993, her only son, Laramiun Byrd, was murdered by a 16-year-old boy named Oshea Israel in Minneapolis, Minnesota. Johnson was understandably devastated by the loss of her son, but she was determined to find a way to move forward and find meaning in her tragedy.

After Israel was convicted of murder, he was sentenced to 25 years in prison. Johnson struggled for years to come to terms with her anger and grief, until one day, she decided to reach out to Israel in prison. She visited him regularly, and over time, they developed a close relationship.

Johnson eventually founded a non-profit organization called "From Death to Life" which aims to help families of homicide victims find healing and reconciliation. She and Israel also started giving joint presentations on the power of forgiveness and reconciliation, sharing their unlikely story of friendship and forgiveness.

In 2010, Johnson and Israel were invited to speak at a TEDx event in Minnesota. Their talk, titled "The Compassionate Witness," was a powerful testament to the power of forgiveness and the human capacity for empathy and connection. Johnson's journey from grief and despair to forgiveness and compassion serves as an inspiration to all those who have suffered loss and are searching for a way to heal.

Joan Didion writes about her experience of grief

Joan Didion is a celebrated American author, known for her personal essays and memoirs. Her work often explores themes of grief and loss, as she has experienced a great deal of both throughout her life.

In 2003, Didion lost her husband, the writer John Gregory Dunne, to a heart attack. The couple had been married for almost forty years and had collaborated on several books together. In her memoir, "The Year of Magical Thinking," Didion writes about her experience of grief in the aftermath of her husband's death.

Didion describes the surreal experience of trying to navigate her day-to-day life while grappling with her overwhelming sense of loss. She writes about the disorienting feeling of walking through her home, which was filled with reminders of her husband's absence. She describes the ways in which grief made her feel physically ill, causing her to lose weight and struggle to sleep.

Despite the enormity of her grief, Didion was able to find moments of solace and connection with others. She writes about the comfort she found in spending time with her daughter, who was also grieving the loss of her father. She also writes about the kindness of friends and strangers who offered their support during this difficult time.

Throughout "The Year of Magical Thinking," Didion reflects on the nature of grief and the ways in which it can transform a person's perspective on the world. She writes about the importance of cherishing the moments we have with loved ones, and the challenges of moving forward after experiencing such a profound loss.

In the end, Didion's story is one of resilience and perseverance in the face of unimaginable tragedy. Through her writing, she has inspired countless readers to confront their own experiences of grief and loss and to find hope and meaning in the midst of adversity.

Chapter Two

Breaking the Chains

Overcoming Addiction and Substance Abuse

The chapter on "Breaking the Chains: Overcoming Addiction and Substance Abuse" will explore the inspiring stories of individuals who overcame addiction and substance abuse. Addiction is a powerful force that can consume a person's life, leaving them feeling hopeless and alone. However, through determination, support, and a desire for change, many people have been able to break free from the chains of addiction and find a new path toward a healthy and fulfilling life.

The chapter will begin by exploring the root causes of addiction and substance abuse, including genetics, environmental factors, and emotional trauma. It will then introduce readers to a range of inspiring individuals who overcame addiction, including celebrities, athletes, and everyday people who battled their way back to sobriety.

The stories shared in this chapter will showcase the

resilience and strength of those who have faced addiction and emerged victorious. These individuals will share their struggles with addiction, the challenges they faced on their road to recovery, and the strategies they used to overcome their addiction and rebuild their lives.

The chapter will also highlight the importance of support systems, including friends, family, and professional resources such as rehab centers, counseling, and support groups. The journey to recovery is not easy, and it often takes a village to help someone overcome addiction and substance abuse.

The chapter will conclude by emphasizing the message of hope, reminding readers that recovery is possible and that no matter how bleak things may seem, there is always a path forward toward a brighter tomorrow. The stories shared in this chapter will inspire and encourage those struggling with addiction to seek help and to never give up on the possibility of a better life.

Exploring the root cause of Addiction and Substance Abuse

Addiction and substance abuse are complex issues that affect millions of people worldwide. In this chapter, we will explore the root causes of addiction and substance abuse, including genetics, environmental factors, and emotional trauma. We will also discuss the inspiring stories of individuals who have overcome addiction and substance abuse and emerged stronger and more resilient.

Addiction and substance abuse often stem from a combination of factors, including genetic predisposition, environmental influences, and emotional trauma. Research has shown that individuals with a family history of addiction are more likely to develop an addiction themselves. Additionally, environmental factors such as peer pressure, availability of drugs or alcohol, and exposure to trauma can all contribute to the development of addiction.

Emotional trauma, such as childhood abuse or neglect, can also be a significant factor in the development of addiction. For many individuals, substance abuse becomes a way to cope with emotional pain or trauma. Over time, however, substance abuse can become a vicious cycle, leading to increased emotional and physical distress, and further perpetuating the addiction.

Despite the challenges of addiction and substance abuse, many individuals have successfully overcome these struggles and gone on to live fulfilling lives. Through determination, support, and a willingness to change, they have broken the chains of addiction and emerged stronger on the other side.

One such inspiring story is that of Sarah, who struggled with alcohol addiction for many years. Despite several unsuccessful attempts to quit, she persisted and eventually found the support she needed to overcome her addiction. With the help of a supportive community and a commitment to self-care, Sarah has now been sober for several years and has transformed her life in countless positive ways.

Another inspiring story is that of David, who struggled with opioid addiction for many years. Despite the devastating impact that his addiction had on his life, David eventually sought help and was able to overcome his addiction through a combination of therapy, medication-assisted treatment, and a strong support network. Today, David is an advocate for addiction recovery and helps others who are struggling with addiction.

These stories of resilience and triumph demonstrate that no matter how challenging addiction and substance abuse may seem, there is always hope for recovery. With the right support and a commitment to change, anyone can break the chains of addiction and emerge stronger on the other side.

Two stories that showcase the resilience and strength of those who have overcome addiction

Anthony Bourdain

Anthony Bourdain was a world-renowned chef, author, and television personality who struggled with addiction for much of his life. He began drinking heavily in his 20s and later developed a cocaine addiction. Bourdain's addiction affected his personal and professional life, leading to the breakdown of his first marriage and the loss of several jobs.

In 1999, Bourdain sought help for his addiction and entered a rehab program. He later wrote about his struggles with addiction in his book "Kitchen Confidential," which became a bestseller. Bourdain went on to have a successful career in the food industry, hosting several popular television shows and writing several more books. He was a vocal advocate for mental health and addiction awareness until his tragic death by suicide in 2018.

Bourdain's story shows that with determination and the right support, it is possible to overcome addiction and build a successful and fulfilling life.

Demi Lovato

Demi Lovato is a singer, actress, and songwriter who has been open about her struggles with addiction and mental health. Lovato began using drugs and alcohol at a young age and was diagnosed with bipolar disorder in her 20s. She has had several publicized relapses and overdoses but has also been vocal about her commitment to sobriety and mental health treatment.

Lovato has used her platform to raise awareness about addiction and mental health issues and has been an advocate for destigmatizing seeking help for these issues.

She has also been open about the challenges of recovery, including the importance of surrounding oneself with a strong support system.

Despite the setbacks she has faced, Lovato has continued to have a successful career in the entertainment industry and has become an important voice for those struggling with addiction and mental health issues.

Both of these stories show that overcoming addiction is a difficult but achievable goal and that with the right support and resources, individuals can move past their struggles and lead fulfilling lives.

The importance of support systems, including friends, family, and professional resources

In the journey toward overcoming addiction and substance abuse, having a strong support system is crucial. It is often said that addiction is a disease of isolation, and it can be incredibly difficult to overcome it without the help of others.

Family and friends can be an important source of support for individuals struggling with addiction. Their love and encouragement can provide the motivation needed to seek treatment and stay on track with recovery. However, it's important to note that not everyone may have a supportive network of family and friends, or they may not feel comfortable sharing their struggles with them.

That's where professional resources such as rehab centers, counseling, and support groups can be incredibly helpful. These resources provide a safe and supportive environment for individuals to address their addiction and work toward recovery. In rehab centers, individuals can receive medically supervised detoxification, as well as therapy and counseling to address the underlying issues that may have led to their addiction. Counseling can also be a valuable resource for those who may not need the structure of a rehab center but still need help and guidance in their journey toward recovery.

Support groups such as Alcoholics Anonymous or Narcotics Anonymous can provide a sense of community and connection with others who have shared similar struggles. These groups provide a non-judgmental space where individuals can share their experiences, receive support and encouragement, and learn from others who have successfully overcome addiction.

It's important to recognize that overcoming addiction is a journey, and it may involve setbacks and challenges along the way. But with the support of family, friends, and professional resources, it is possible to break the chains of addiction and achieve long-term recovery.

Here are a few examples of individuals who overcame addiction and the important role that support systems played in their recovery:

Robert Downey Jr.: The Hollywood actor struggled with addiction for years, eventually hitting rock bottom in the late 1990s. He was in and out of rehab and even served time in prison. However, he was determined to turn his life around and sought help from friends and family. He eventually found success in his career, starring in blockbuster films like Iron Man and The Avengers.

Eric Clapton: The legendary musician battled addiction to drugs and alcohol, and even lost his young son to a tragic accident. With the support of his family, friends, and a 12-step program, he was able to overcome his addiction and continue making music.

Russell Brand: The comedian and actor has been sober since 2003 after battling addiction to drugs and alcohol for many years. He emphasizes the importance of support systems in recovery, including rehab centers, 12-step programs, and therapy.

These individuals all faced their own unique challenges with addiction, but their stories demonstrate the power of support systems in overcoming adversity and achieving long-term recovery that can seem dark and hopeless, it's important to remember that recovery is always possible, even for those who have struggled with addiction and substance abuse. It's a message of hope that many people need to hear, especially when they feel like they're at their lowest point.

The Message of Hope

There are countless stories of people who have overcome addiction and substance abuse, and these stories are filled with hope and inspiration. They remind us that no matter how bad things may seem, there is always a way out and that we are never alone in our struggles.

One important message of hope is that recovery is possible at any stage of addiction. Whether you've been struggling with substance abuse for years or have just started to realize that you have a problem, there is always a way forward. It's never too late to seek help, to start making positive changes in your life, and to work toward a healthier, happier future.

Another important message of hope is that there are countless resources available to help people on their journey to recovery. From counseling and therapy to support groups and rehab centers, there is a wide range of options available to those who are struggling with addiction. These resources provide guidance, support, and a safe space for people to work through their struggles and build a brighter future.

Perhaps most importantly, the message of hope reminds us that we are not defined by our past struggles. No matter what we may have gone through, we have the power to change our lives and create a better future for ourselves. We are capable of healing, of growing, and of finding joy and fulfillment in our lives.

Jamie Lee Curtis, the actress, struggled with addiction to painkillers for many years and even stole pills from friends and family members to support her habit. However, she eventually sought help and got sober, and has remained committed to living a healthy, drug-free life ever since. She has spoken publicly about her struggles with addiction and the importance of seeking help for those who are struggling.

Eminem: The rapper has been open about his struggles with addiction to prescription medication and how it almost cost him his life. He eventually sought help and has been sober since 2008. He uses his music as a platform to encourage others to seek help for their own addiction struggles.

Ultimately, the message of hope is a powerful one, and

it's one that can help inspire and motivate those who are struggling with addiction and substance abuse. It reminds us that we are never alone in our struggles and that with the right support, resources, and mindset, we can overcome any obstacle and create a brighter future for ourselves.

Chapter Three

Fighting Against the Odds

Overcoming Health Challenges

This chapter tells the inspiring stories of individuals who have faced serious health challenges and have emerged victorious through their determination and resilience.

The chapter begins with an exploration of the various physical and mental health challenges that people can face, from chronic illness to debilitating injuries and mental health disorders. It highlights the importance of early detection, seeking professional help, and developing a support system to overcome these challenges.

The chapter then shares a series of individual stories that illustrate the power of perseverance in the face of adversity.

The Story of Christopher Reeve

Christopher Reeve was an American actor best known for his role as Superman in the popular film franchise. In 1995,

Reeve's life was forever changed when he was thrown from his horse during an equestrian competition and suffered a spinal cord injury, leaving him paralyzed from the neck down.

Despite the devastating nature of his injury, Reeve refused to let it define him. Instead, he became an advocate for spinal cord injury research and a symbol of hope and inspiration for those living with paralysis. Reeve underwent years of grueling physical therapy and rehabilitation and eventually regained some use of his arms and hands.

Reeve's resilience and determination in the face of adversity were truly remarkable. He refused to be defined by his disability and instead focused on what he could still do rather than what he could not. He became a powerful voice for the disability community, advocating for increased research funding and better access to care for those with spinal cord injuries.

In 1998, Reeve founded the Christopher Reeve Foundation, which funds research and provides resources and support for people with spinal cord injuries and their families. He also worked tirelessly to raise awareness about the need for better treatments and a cure for paralysis.

Sadly, Reeve passed away in 2004 from complications related to his injury. However, his legacy lives on through the foundation he created and the countless lives he touched with his message of hope, resilience, and determination. Reeve's story is a powerful reminder that no matter what challenges we face in life, we have the power to overcome them and make a positive impact in the world.

Lance Armstrong's Story

Lance Armstrong is a former professional cyclist who was diagnosed with testicular cancer in 1996, at the age of 25. The cancer had spread to his brain and lungs, and he was given less than a 50% chance of survival. Despite the grim prognosis, Armstrong was determined to fight the disease with all his might.

Armstrong underwent surgery to remove the cancerous testicle and then underwent several rounds of chemotherapy. During this time, he suffered from intense physical and emotional pain, and at times felt like giving up. However, he was inspired by the support of his family and friends, as well as the other cancer patients he met during his treatment.

After completing his treatment, Armstrong decided to return to professional cycling and set his sights on winning the Tour de France, the most prestigious race in the sport. His first attempt in 1999 was successful, and he went on to win the race a record-breaking seven times in a row.

Armstrong's story is one of incredible resilience and determination in the face of adversity. Despite being diagnosed with a life-threatening illness, he refused to let it defeat him. Instead, he used it as a catalyst to achieve even greater things, both in his personal life and in his career. Armstrong's message of hope and perseverance continues to inspire countless people around the world who are facing their own battles with cancer or other health challenges.

The Story of Randy Pausch

Randy Pausch was a professor of computer science at Carnegie Mellon University who became famous for his inspiring Last Lecture, titled "Really Achieving Your Childhood Dreams," which he delivered after being diagnosed with terminal pancreatic cancer.

Pausch was only 47 years old when he received the devastating news that he had just a few months to live. Instead of wallowing in self-pity, he decided to use his remaining time to share his wisdom and experience with others. He gave a lecture to his students that quickly became an internet sensation, and he was invited to appear on numerous talk shows and give keynote speeches to audiences around the world.

Pausch's Last Lecture was a moving and inspiring account of his life, his dreams, and the lessons he had learned along the way. He talked about the importance of perseverance, the value of hard work and determination, and the need to focus on what really matters in life. He encouraged his audience to follow their own dreams and to never give up, even in the face of seemingly insurmountable obstacles.

Pausch's message resonated with millions of people around the world, and his book, "The Last Lecture," became a bestseller.

Even after his death, Pausch's legacy continued to inspire others, and his story is a testament to the power of the human spirit in overcoming adversity.

Chapter Four

A Different Kind of Strength

Overcoming Disability and Physical Limitations

Physical disabilities can seem like insurmountable obstacles, but those who have overcome them have proven that they are no match for the human spirit. This chapter explores the stories of individuals who have faced physical limitations head-on, and in doing so, have achieved remarkable feats.

Section 1: The Power of the Mind- Overcoming Psychological Limits

When faced with a physical disability, the mind can become an individual's greatest asset or worst enemy. This section explores the stories of individuals who have overcome psychological limitations and found strength within themselves.

Stephen Hawking's Story

Stephen Hawking is one of the most well-known and respected physicists and cosmologists of the modern era, despite being diagnosed with a debilitating disease at a young age. Hawking was born in Oxford, England, in 1942, and was a promising student from a young age. However, at the age of 21, he was diagnosed with a rare form of motor neuron disease called amyotrophic lateral sclerosis (ALS), which gradually robbed him of his ability to move and speak.

Despite this devastating diagnosis, Hawking refused to let his condition hold him back. He continued his studies, earning a Ph.D. in cosmology from the University of Cambridge in 1966, and went on to make groundbreaking discoveries about the nature of the universe. He developed a theory of cosmology known as the "Hawking radiation," which demonstrated that black holes could actually emit energy and particles.

He also authored several best-selling books, including "A Brief History of Time," which made complex physics concepts accessible to a wider audience.

Throughout his life, Hawking relied on a motorized wheelchair and a computerized voice synthesizer to communicate, as he had lost the ability to speak and move on his own. However, he refused to be defined by his disability and instead used his platform to advocate for people with disabilities and promote scientific understanding. He was known for his quick wit, his engaging lectures, and his determination to push the boundaries of human knowledge.

Hawking passed away in 2018, but his legacy as a brilliant scientist and an inspiration to people with disabilities lives on. His story demonstrates that even in the face of overwhelming physical limitations, it is possible to achieve great things and leave a lasting impact on the world.

The Story of Marla Runyan

Marla Runyan is an American track and field athlete who overcame visual impairment to achieve great success in her sport. Born in 1969 in Santa Maria, California, Marla was diagnosed with Stargardt's disease, a form of macular degeneration that causes progressive vision loss, when she was nine years old. Despite her vision impairment, Marla was an active child and started running in middle school. She continued to pursue her passion for running in high school and college, and in 1996 she was named to the US Olympic team for the 1500-meter race.

At the Atlanta Olympics that year, Marla finished eighth in her event, an incredible achievement for an athlete with visual impairment. She went on to compete in several other international events, including the Pan American Games and the World Championships, winning multiple gold and silver medals. In 2000, Marla set a new American record in the 5000-meter race and was named the USATF Athlete of the Year.

Marla's success in athletics is a testament to her hard work, dedication, and determination to overcome the physical limitations imposed by her disability. She trained tirelessly, often running alone on a track with no guide or coach, using a special auditory device to help her stay on course. She also developed her other senses, such as hearing and touch, to help compensate for her visual impairment.

Marla's achievements have not only inspired others with visual impairments to pursue their dreams but also raised awareness about the capabilities of people with disabilities. She has become a role model for people around the world, showing that with perseverance and hard work, anyone can overcome physical limitations and achieve great things.

Section 2: Making the Impossible Possible-Overcoming Physical Limits

This section explores the stories of individuals who have overcome physical limitations through sheer determination and perseverance.

Bethany Hamilton's Story

Bethany Hamilton is a professional surfer who was born on February 8, 1990, in Lihue, Hawaii. At the age of 13, she was attacked by a 14-foot tiger shark while surfing off the coast of Kauai. The attack resulted in the loss of her left arm, which could have ended her surfing career. However, Bethany refused to give up her passion for surfing and was determined to overcome the adversity she faced.

With the help of her family and friends, Bethany slowly began to regain her strength and started surfing again just one month after the attack. She had to relearn how to paddle, duck dive, and catch waves with only one arm, which required an incredible amount of perseverance and determination.

Despite her injury, Bethany continued to compete in surf competitions and eventually became a professional surfer. In 2004, she won her first national title and went on to win several other titles over the years, including the NSSA National Championship in 2005 and 2007.

Bethany's story of overcoming adversity has inspired many people around the world, and she has become a role model for those facing similar challenges. She has also used her platform to raise awareness for shark conservation and to encourage people to pursue their dreams no matter what obstacles they may face. Bethany's resilience, strength, and determination in the face of adversity serve as a reminder that anything is possible with the right mindset and support system.

Nick Vujicic's Story

Nick Vujicic is a motivational speaker and author who was born without arms or legs due to a rare condition called tetra-amelia syndrome. Despite facing numerous physical and emotional challenges throughout his life, Vujicic has become a well-known advocate for people with disabilities and a source of inspiration for millions around the world.

Growing up, Vujicic struggled with feelings of isolation and depression, often feeling like he didn't fit in with other kids. However, he eventually found purpose and meaning in his life through his faith in God and began sharing his story and message of hope with others.

Vujicic has gone on to speak to thousands of people in over 60 countries, spreading his message of resilience, perseverance, and overcoming adversity. He has also written several books, including "Life Without Limits" and "Unstoppable," which have inspired countless readers to push through their own challenges and live their best lives.

Despite the physical limitations he faces, Vujicic has accomplished a great deal in his life. He is married with four children and is an accomplished swimmer, surfer, and golfer. His story serves as a powerful reminder that with determination and a positive attitude, anything is possible.

Section 3: Adaptive Sports- Overcoming Physical Limits Through Sports

Sports can be a powerful tool for those with physical disabilities, allowing them to push their limits and overcome physical obstacles.

The Story of Tatyana McFadden

Tatyana McFadden is a Russian-born American Paralympian who has overcome many challenges and physical limitations in her life. She was born with spina bifida, a condition that affects the spinal cord and left her paralyzed from the waist down. Her birth mother abandoned her at a local orphanage in St. Petersburg, Russia, where she spent the first six years of her life.

Despite her circumstances, Tatyana was determined to overcome her disability and make the most of her life. She was eventually adopted by an American woman named Debbie McFadden, who brought her to the United States and raised her in Maryland. Tatyana began playing sports at a young age, and she quickly discovered her talent for wheelchair racing.

Over the years, Tatyana has become one of the most successful and decorated athletes in Paralympic history. She has won numerous gold medals and set multiple world records in wheelchair racing events at the Paralympic Games and other international competitions. In addition to her success in athletics, Tatyana has also become a prominent disability rights advocate and a role model for others with disabilities.

Tatyana's story is a testament to the power of perseverance and determination in overcoming physical limitations. Despite facing numerous obstacles throughout her life, she refused to let her disability define her or hold her back. Through hard work and dedication, she has achieved remarkable success and become a true inspiration to others.

Jim Abbott's Story

Jim Abbott's story is one of overcoming physical adversity to achieve greatness. Born without a right hand, Abbott faced numerous challenges growing up. However, he was determined to play baseball, and through hard work and dedication, he became one of the best pitchers in the game.

Abbott's story is one of perseverance in the face of adversity. Despite being born with a disability, he refused to let it hold him back. He learned to pitch using his left hand, and he practiced tirelessly until he became a standout player.

Abbott's talent on the field earned him a scholarship to the University of Michigan, where he was a standout pitcher. In 1988, he was selected by the California Angels in the first round of the MLB draft. He went on to play for several other teams over the course of his career, including the New York Yankees and the Chicago White Sox.

Throughout his career, Abbott proved that he was more than just a pitcher with a disability. He was a talented athlete who was able to compete at the highest levels of the game. He even threw a no-hitter for the Yankees in 1993, a feat that few pitchers ever achieve.

Abbott's story serves as an inspiration to anyone who has faced adversity in their lives. It is a reminder that with hard work, determination, and a never-give-up attitude, anything is possible. Despite being born with a disability, Abbott was able to achieve greatness in his chosen field, and he continues to inspire others to this day.

These stories serve as a reminder that even in the face of the most daunting health challenges, there is always hope for recovery and renewed strength. They highlight the importance of staying positive, seeking help, and never giving up on one's dreams and goals.

The Story of Amy Purdy

Amy Purdy is an American snowboarder, actress, model, and motivational speaker who overcame great odds after losing both of her legs below the knee at the age of 19 due to bacterial meningitis. Despite the challenges she faced, Purdy remained determined to pursue her passion for snowboarding, and with the help of prosthetic legs, she went on to become a successful professional athlete.

Purdy's journey to success was not an easy one. After her amputation, she struggled with depression and the loss of her identity as an athlete. However, with the support of her family and friends, she began to regain her confidence and focus on her future. She learned how to snowboard again, and with her newfound passion for the sport, she set her sights on competing in the Paralympic Games.

In 2014, Purdy represented the United States at the Paralympic Winter Games in Sochi, Russia, and won a bronze medal in snowboarding. She has since become a champion for adaptive sports and a role model for others facing adversity.

Beyond her athletic accomplishments, Purdy has also

become an advocate for the disabled community and a motivational speaker. She has shared her story with audiences around the world, encouraging others to embrace their unique abilities and pursue their dreams, no matter the obstacles they may face.

Pascale Honore's Story

Pascale Honore is an Australian woman who, despite being paralyzed from the waist down, was able to fulfill her dream of surfing with the help of a good friend.

In 1995, Pascale was in a car accident that left her paralyzed. She was devastated by the accident and struggled to find meaning in her life. As someone who loved the ocean and surfing, she felt particularly lost without the ability to enjoy the waves.

That all changed when Pascale met Tyron Swan, a local surfer who had grown up in the area and knew the waves well. Tyron had been surfing since he was a child and was passionate about the sport. When he learned that Pascale wanted to surf, he was determined to help her.

At first, Tyron would take Pascale out on his back, carrying her out to the waves and then helping her onto his surfboard. But as Pascale's confidence grew, she began using a specially designed board that allowed her to lie down and paddle with her arms.

With Tyron's help, Pascale was able to experience the thrill of riding the waves once again. Her spirit was renewed, and she began to see her life in a different light.

She realized that her disability did not have to define her and that she could still do the things she loved with a little help.

Pascale's story is a testament to the power of the human spirit and the importance of perseverance in the face of adversity. Despite facing a significant obstacle, she refused to give up on her dream and was able to find a way to make it a reality. Her story serves as an inspiration to anyone who has faced a similar challenge and struggled to find their way forward.

The Story of Jillian Mercado's

Jillian Mercado is a fashion model and disability activist who has overcome numerous health challenges to become a leading figure in the fashion industry. Born in New York City in 1987, Mercado was diagnosed with spastic muscular dystrophy as a child, a condition that causes progressive muscle weakness and tightness.

Despite the challenges she faced growing up, Mercado always had a love of fashion and style and began to pursue a career in modeling after being scouted by a fashion photographer on Facebook. However, she found that the fashion industry was not always welcoming to people with disabilities, and often lacked inclusivity and diversity.

Undeterred, Mercado continued to pursue her dreams and eventually caught the attention of iconic fashion designer and activist, Diesel's artistic director Nicola Formichetti, who cast her in a campaign for the brand in

2014. This was a groundbreaking moment in the fashion industry, as it was one of the first times a model with a physical disability had been featured in a major fashion campaign.

Since then, Mercado has continued to push for greater inclusivity and diversity in the fashion industry, speaking out about the need for better representation of people with disabilities and other marginalized groups. She has worked with major brands such as Target, Olay, and Tommy Hilfiger, and has been featured in publications such as Vogue and Glamour.

Through her work and advocacy, Mercado has become an inspiration to many, showing that with hard work, determination, and a refusal to be held back by societal expectations or limitations, anyone can overcome adversity and achieve their dreams.

The stories of these individuals demonstrate the incredible power of the human spirit to overcome physical limitations. Whether it's through the power of the mind, sheer determination, or adaptive sports, these individuals have shown that nothing can hold them back from achieving their dreams. They are a testament to the fact that strength comes in many different forms and that overcoming adversity is not just about physical ability, but also about mental fortitude and emotional resilience.

Chapter Five

The Road to Recovery

Overcoming Mental Illness and Trauma

Overcoming mental illness and trauma can be one of the most difficult challenges a person can face. Whether it's a debilitating mental illness like schizophrenia or bipolar disorder, or the aftermath of a traumatic event like abuse, assault, or combat, the journey to recovery can be long and arduous, but it is a journey that is worth taking. It takes courage, perseverance, and a willingness to seek help and support.

This journey can be one of the most rewarding and transformative journeys a person can take. With the right support, tools, and mindset, individuals can learn to manage their symptoms, heal their wounds, and reclaim their lives.

In this chapter, we will explore the inspiring stories of individuals who have faced mental illness and trauma and emerged stronger and more resilient and offers hope and guidance for those on the same path.

The Story of Kevin Hines

Kevin Hines is a motivational speaker and mental health advocate who has become a leading voice in the fight against suicide. Hines was diagnosed with bipolar disorder in his early 20s, and for years he struggled with the disease, experiencing severe mood swings, depression, and suicidal thoughts.

In 2000, at the age of 19, Hines attempted suicide by jumping off the Golden Gate Bridge in San Francisco. Miraculously, he survived the fall but suffered multiple broken bones and internal injuries. During his long and painful recovery, Hines realized that he wanted to use his experience to help others struggling with mental illness and suicidal ideation.

Since then, Hines has become a highly sought-after speaker, sharing his story of survival and hope with audiences around the world. He has given talks at universities, hospitals, and mental health conferences, and has appeared on numerous television and radio programs.

In addition to his speaking engagements, Hines is also an advocate for mental health policy reform. He has worked with lawmakers in California and other states to pass legislation aimed at preventing suicide and improving mental health care.

Despite the challenges he has faced, Hines remains a powerful example of resilience and perseverance. He continues to inspire others with his message of hope, reminding them that no matter how dark things may seem, recovery is always possible.

Lena Dunham's Story

Lena Dunham is a writer, producer, and actress who is best known for creating and starring in the HBO series "Girls." Despite her success, Dunham has struggled with mental illness throughout her life.

Dunham has been open about her experiences with anxiety and obsessive-compulsive disorder (OCD). In her memoir "Not That Kind of Girl," she writes about how her OCD manifested itself in various ways, including a fear of contamination and a need for symmetry and order.

Dunham has also been diagnosed with depression, which she has described as feeling like a "constant low-grade fever." In interviews and essays, she has discussed how therapy, medication, and self-care have been important tools for managing her mental health.

Dunham's willingness to share her struggles with mental illness has been an important part of her advocacy work. She has spoken out about the importance of mental health care and the need to reduce the stigma around mental illness. In 2015, she launched a campaign called Lenny Letters to provide a platform for women's voices, including those who are often marginalized due to mental illness or other factors. Through her work, Dunham has shown that it is possible to thrive while managing mental health challenges and that seeking help is a sign of strength, not weakness.

The Story of Brandon Marshall

Brandon Marshall is a former NFL wide receiver who has spoken out about his struggles with borderline personality disorder (BPD) and is now a mental health advocate. Marshall was drafted in 2006 by the Denver Broncos and played for several other teams, including the Chicago Bears and New York Jets.

Despite his successful football career, Marshall struggled with intense emotional highs and lows, impulsivity, and difficulty with interpersonal relationships. After being arrested several times and receiving multiple diagnoses and treatments, he was finally diagnosed with BPD in 2011.

Marshall has since become a vocal advocate for mental health awareness, sharing his story to reduce the stigma around mental illness and encourage others to seek help.

He founded the Brandon Marshall Foundation, which focuses on increasing awareness and access to mental health resources. He has also been involved in various initiatives to promote mental health education and support, including the NFL's "My Cause My Cleats" campaign, which allows players to wear custom cleats to raise awareness for their chosen causes.

Through his advocacy work, Marshall has shown that with the right support and treatment, it is possible to overcome mental health challenges and lead a fulfilling life.

Michael Phelps's Story

Michael Phelps is a retired American swimmer and the most decorated Olympian of all time, with a total of 28 medals, including 23 gold medals. Despite his immense success in the pool, Phelps has been open about his struggles with mental health and substance abuse.

In 2014, Phelps was arrested for driving under the influence and subsequently entered a treatment program for alcohol addiction. He has also spoken publicly about his struggles with depression, which led him to contemplate suicide at one point.

However, Phelps has become a powerful advocate for mental health awareness and has used his platform to encourage others to seek help. In 2017, he teamed up with the mental health app Talkspace to promote the benefits of online therapy.

Phelps has also been open about the role that his family and support system played in his recovery. He credits his wife and children for giving him a sense of purpose and helping him stay on track.

Through his story, Phelps demonstrates that even the most accomplished and successful individuals can struggle with mental health issues and addiction. However, with the right support and resources, recovery and resilience are possible.

The Story of Amanda Nguyen

Amanda Nguyen is a rape survivor and founder of Rise, a nonprofit organization that advocates for the rights of sexual assault survivors. Nguyen's experience with the criminal justice system following her assault led her to advocate for policy changes to improve the treatment of survivors.

After Nguyen was sexually assaulted in 2013, she went to the hospital and underwent a rape kit examination but was then told that the kit would be destroyed after just six months if she didn't pay to have it stored. This was due to a loophole in the law that allowed for rape kits to be destroyed after a certain amount of time if the victim didn't pay for storage.

This led Nguyen to launch a petition to extend the statute of limitations for rape kits and to create a national standard for their storage.

Her petition led to the passage of the Sexual Assault Survivors' Rights Act, which provides basic rights to sexual assault survivors, including the right to free rape kit exams and to have the kit preserved for the duration of the statute of limitations.

In addition to her advocacy work with Rise, Nguyen has also been recognized for her activism with awards such as the Forbes 30 Under 30 list and the Presidential Public Service Award.

Jaycee Dugard's Story

Jaycee Dugard is a survivor of one of the most horrific and long-term kidnappings in American history. In 1991, when she was just 11 years old, Dugard was abducted by Phillip Garrido while she was walking to the school bus stop in South Lake Tahoe, California.

Garrido held Dugard captive in a hidden compound in his backyard, where he and his wife Nancy repeatedly raped and abused her for 18 years.

During her captivity, Dugard gave birth to two daughters, who were also held captive with her. Despite the unimaginable trauma she experienced, Dugard was able to find moments of hope and strength, and she never lost sight of the possibility of one day being reunited with her family.

In 2009, Garrido's suspicious behavior led to an investigation that ultimately led to Dugard's rescue. She was able to reconnect with her family and begin the long and difficult process of healing and rebuilding her life.

Dugard's story is a testament to the resilience of the human spirit and the power of hope in the face of unimaginable adversity. She has since become an advocate for victims of kidnapping and sexual abuse and has worked to raise awareness of the importance of support and resources for survivors of trauma.

The Story of Mariel Hemingway

Mariel Hemingway is an American actress, author, and mental health advocate who has overcome a traumatic family history to find strength and resilience in her own life. She was born into the Hemingway family, known for their literary and artistic contributions to American culture, but also for their struggles with mental illness and addiction.

Mariel's grandfather, Ernest Hemingway, took his own life when she was just one year old, and her father, Jack Hemingway, suffered from severe depression and ultimately died by suicide as well. Mariel herself struggled with anxiety, depression, and addiction from a young age, but was determined to overcome her family's legacy of mental illness and forge her own path.

As a teenager, Mariel began her career as an actress and quickly rose to fame with her breakout role in the film "Manhattan" directed by Woody Allen. However, behind the scenes, she was struggling with her mental health and often turned to drugs and alcohol to cope. It wasn't until she met her husband, Stephen Crisman, that she began to confront her issues head-on and seek treatment for her addiction and mental health challenges.

Through therapy, meditation, and a commitment to sobriety, Mariel was able to turn her life around and become a vocal advocate for mental health awareness and suicide prevention.

She has written several books on the subject, including "Finding My Balance: A Memoir with Yoga" and "Out Came the Sun: Overcoming the Legacy of Mental Illness,

Addiction, and Suicide in My Family," and has become a sought-after speaker on the topic.

Mariel's story is a powerful reminder that it's never too late to seek help and overcome even the most challenging of obstacles. Despite the traumas and struggles she faced in her early life, she was able to find the strength within herself to heal and build a fulfilling and purposeful life.

These stories of resilience and triumph over mental illness and trauma remind us that recovery is possible and that there is always hope. With the right support and resources, individuals can overcome even the most difficult challenges and emerge stronger and more resilient than ever before.

Chapter Six

Learning to Adapt

Overcoming Career Setbacks and Job Loss

No one plans for setbacks and job loss. It is an unexpected turn of events that can leave you feeling lost and unsure of the future. It is during these moments that resilience and adaptability are essential.

Learning to adapt in the face of career setbacks and job loss can be one of the most difficult challenges a person can face. The loss of a job, particularly in today's uncertain economy, can be financially and emotionally devastating. It can uproot your sense of stability, confidence, and self-worth. Yet, many people have overcome such challenges by learning to adapt to the new realities of their lives. They have discovered that a job loss or career setback can also present an opportunity to reinvent oneself, pursue a new path, or make significant changes to their lives that they may have been hesitant to make otherwise.

In this chapter, we explore the inspiring stories of

individuals who overcame career setbacks and job loss, demonstrating the importance of staying positive, being proactive, and learning to adapt in the face of adversity.

J.K. Rowling's Story

J.K. Rowling's story is one of the most well-known examples of overcoming career setbacks and achieving incredible success. Rowling was a struggling single mother living in poverty in Edinburgh, Scotland, when she first had the idea for the Harry Potter series. She spent several years writing the first book in the series, "Harry Potter and the Philosopher's Stone," all while dealing with the death of her mother, a divorce, and financial struggles.

When Rowling completed the manuscript for "Harry Potter and the Philosopher's Stone," she sent it to several publishers, all of whom rejected it. However, a small publishing house in London eventually agreed to publish the book, and it was an immediate success.

The book and its subsequent sequels became a cultural phenomenon, selling over 500 million copies worldwide and inspiring a massive film franchise.

Despite her incredible success, Rowling faced additional setbacks in her career. In 2013, she released "The Casual Vacancy," her first novel aimed at adult audiences, which received mixed reviews. Additionally, her pseudonymous crime novels, published under the name Robert Galbraith, were initially met with a lukewarm reception.

However, Rowling persevered and continued to write

and publish. In recent years, she has become an outspoken advocate for social justice issues, using her platform to speak out against inequality and support causes such as women's rights and LGBTQ+ rights. Rowling's story is a testament to the power of resilience and determination in the face of adversity.

The Story of Walt Disney

Walt Disney is a well-known figure in the entertainment industry, famous for his creation of beloved characters like Mickey Mouse and his development of Disneyland, the world's first theme park. However, Disney's path to success was not an easy one, and he faced numerous setbacks and failures along the way.

Disney started his career as a commercial artist, creating cartoons and advertisements for local businesses. He eventually moved to Hollywood, where he tried to sell his cartoon ideas to various studios but was met with rejection after rejection. Undeterred, Disney decided to create his own animation studio with his brother Roy.

Their first major creation was Oswald the Lucky Rabbit, which was a hit with audiences but unfortunately, they lost the rights to the character due to a contract dispute. This setback could have been the end of the Disney brothers' dream, but they refused to give up. Walt came up with the concept of Mickey Mouse and debuted the character in a cartoon called "Steamboat Willie" in 1928. The rest is history.

Disney continued to face challenges throughout his career, but he always found a way to adapt and innovate. When he was unable to secure financing for Disneyland, he turned to television and created the "Disneyland" show to promote his park. When his animators went on strike, he hired new talent and developed a new technique for animating films. His resilience and determination ultimately led to the creation of one of the world's most successful entertainment companies, inspiring generations of creative people and entrepreneurs.

Oprah Winfrey's Story

Oprah Winfrey is a media mogul, talk show host, actress, and philanthropist who has become an icon of success and inspiration. She was born in rural Mississippi in 1954 and faced significant adversity in her childhood, including poverty, sexual abuse, and a lack of familial stability. Despite these challenges, Oprah excelled in school and won a full scholarship to Tennessee State University, where she majored in communication.

In 1976, Oprah moved to Baltimore to co-anchor the evening news, and she quickly gained popularity for her engaging and relatable style. In 1983, she moved to Chicago to host a morning talk show called "AM Chicago," which eventually became "The Oprah Winfrey Show." The show's format was groundbreaking, with Oprah inviting guests to share their personal stories and struggles and providing a platform for experts to share their knowledge on a variety of topics. The show became a massive success and aired for

25 seasons, making Oprah one of the most influential and wealthy people in the world.

Despite her success, Oprah faced numerous setbacks and challenges throughout her career. In 2011, she launched a cable television network called the Oprah Winfrey Network (OWN), which struggled in its early years and faced criticism from the media. However, Oprah persevered and worked to improve the network's programming, eventually leading it to become profitable and successful.

Throughout her career, Oprah has also been open about her struggles with weight and has inspired millions of people through her personal journey of weight loss and self-acceptance. She has also been a vocal advocate for mental health and has spoken candidly about her experiences with depression and anxiety.

In addition to her media career, Oprah is also a dedicated philanthropist, supporting a variety of causes including education, health, and women's empowerment. She has donated millions of dollars to charitable organizations and established the Oprah Winfrey Leadership Academy for Girls in South Africa, which provides education and leadership training to disadvantaged girls.

Oprah's story is a testament to the power of resilience and adaptability in the face of adversity. Despite facing numerous obstacles throughout her life, she has continued to pursue her passions and use her platform to inspire and empower others. Her success is a reminder that setbacks and failures are not the end, but rather an opportunity for growth and transformation.

The Story of Steve Jobs

Steve Jobs was a visionary entrepreneur and innovator who co-founded Apple Inc., one of the world's most successful and iconic companies. However, Jobs' journey was not without setbacks and challenges. In 1985, he was famously ousted from Apple, the company he had helped create, due to disagreements with the board of directors. This was a major blow for Jobs, who had invested a lot of time, energy, and passion into building the company.

After leaving Apple, Jobs founded NeXT Computer, a company that specialized in creating high-end workstations for businesses and universities. Although the company struggled at first, Jobs remained focused on his vision and continued to innovate. NeXT eventually caught the attention of Apple, which acquired the company in 1997.

Jobs' return to Apple marked the beginning of a new era of success for the company. He was instrumental in the development of the iMac, iPod, iPhone, and iPad, which revolutionized the computer, music, and mobile phone industries. Jobs' innovative approach to design and technology changed the way we interact with digital devices, and his legacy continues to inspire and shape the tech industry today.

Throughout his career, Jobs faced many challenges, but he remained resilient and focused on his goals. He was a visionary leader who believed in taking risks and pursuing big ideas, even when others doubted him. His determination and perseverance are an inspiration to anyone facing career setbacks or challenges.

The Story of Vera Wang

Vera Wang is a renowned fashion designer who has made a name for herself in the highly competitive and challenging world of fashion. However, Vera's path to success was not always smooth, and she had to overcome several setbacks and challenges to reach where she is today.

Vera started her career as a figure skater and was even a member of the US Olympic team. However, after failing to make it to the Olympics, she decided to pursue a career in fashion. She started as an assistant at Vogue and later moved to Ralph Lauren, where she worked for 17 years and eventually became the senior fashion editor.

Despite her success at Ralph Lauren, Vera still had bigger aspirations and decided to start her own fashion label. She launched her eponymous label in 1990, but the first few years were tough, and her designs did not receive the desired recognition. However, Vera did not give up and continued to work hard to refine her designs and build her brand.

Her breakthrough came when she designed a wedding dress for figure skater Nancy Kerrigan for the 1992 Olympics. The dress received widespread attention and recognition, and Vera's brand began to gain traction. Since then, she has designed wedding dresses for several high-profile clients, including Chelsea Clinton, Kim Kardashian, and Victoria Beckham.

Despite her success, Vera has had to adapt and evolve her brand to stay relevant in the constantly changing fashion industry. She has expanded her line to include ready-to-wear, fragrance, home goods, and even bridal registries.

Vera Wang's story is a testament to the power of perseverance, hard work, and adaptation. Despite facing setbacks and challenges, she remained determined to achieve her goals and build a successful career in the competitive world of fashion.

Jack Ma's Story

Jack Ma, also known as Ma Yun, is a Chinese entrepreneur and one of the richest men in the world. He is the co-founder and former executive chairman of Alibaba Group, one of the largest e-commerce companies in the world.

Ma grew up poor in Hangzhou, China, and struggled in school, failing his college entrance exam twice. After graduation, he applied for dozens of jobs and was rejected from all of them, including KFC, which had just opened its first location in China. However, Ma remained persistent and eventually found work as an English teacher, earning just $12 a month.

In 1995, Ma visited the United States for the first time and was introduced to the internet. He recognized the potential of the internet for business and realized that there were no Chinese websites at the time. He founded his first company, China Pages, which created websites for Chinese businesses.

Ma's big break came in 1999 when he founded Alibaba.com, a business-to-business e-commerce platform that connected Chinese manufacturers with overseas buyers. The company grew quickly and eventually expanded into consumer e-commerce with the launch of Taobao and Tmall.

Despite facing setbacks and challenges along the way, such as fierce competition from other companies and regulatory issues, Ma never gave up. He focused on innovation and expansion, and Alibaba became one of the most valuable companies in the world.

In 2019, Ma retired from Alibaba Group, but he continues to be an influential figure in the business world and an advocate for entrepreneurship. He has also dedicated himself to philanthropy and environmental causes, founding the Jack Ma Foundation and the Paradise International Foundation

The Story of Sheryl Sandberg

Sheryl Sandberg is an American technology executive and author, best known for her work as the Chief Operating Officer (COO) of Facebook. She was born in 1969 in Washington, D.C., and grew up in North Miami Beach, Florida.

After earning her bachelor's degree in economics from Harvard University in 1991, Sandberg went on to earn her MBA from Harvard Business School in 1995. She began her career in business as a management consultant at McKinsey & Company before joining Google in 2001 as Vice President of Global Online Sales and Operations.

In 2008, Sandberg was recruited by Facebook's CEO, Mark Zuckerberg, to become the company's COO. At the time, Facebook was still a relatively small social networking site, and Sandberg's experience and expertise helped to scale the company's operations and revenue streams. Under her leadership, Facebook's user base grew from around 100 million to over 2 billion.

In 2012, Sandberg published her first book, "Lean In: Women, Work, and the Will to Lead," which addressed issues of gender equality in the workplace and inspired a global movement. In 2015, Sandberg faced a personal setback when her husband, Dave Goldberg, unexpectedly passed away while the couple was on vacation in Mexico.

In the aftermath of her husband's death, Sandberg became a vocal advocate for resilience and overcoming adversity. She continued to lead Facebook while also devoting time to personal growth and healing. In 2017, she published her second book, "Option B: Facing Adversity, Building Resilience, and Finding Joy," which was co-written with psychologist and grief expert Adam Grant. The book drew on Sandberg's own experiences and offered insights and advice on how to recover from loss and overcome setbacks.

Sandberg's story is one of perseverance, resilience, and adaptability. She has faced both personal and professional challenges throughout her career but has always found ways to learn from her experiences and move forward. Through her leadership at Facebook and her advocacy for women's rights and resilience, she has become a role model for many.

Howard Schultz's Story

Howard Schultz is a successful entrepreneur and businessman who is best known for his role as the chairman and CEO of Starbucks, the world's largest coffeehouse chain. Schultz was born in Brooklyn, New York in 1953 and grew up in public housing in Canarsie. After graduating from Northern Michigan University, Schultz worked as a salesman for Xerox before becoming a general manager at a Swedish housewares company called Hammarplast.

In 1981, Schultz visited a Starbucks coffee shop in Seattle and was struck by the quality of the coffee and the community atmosphere. He joined the company as its director of marketing a year later and convinced the founders to start serving espresso drinks, which were popular in Europe but virtually unknown in the US at the time. Schultz left Starbucks in 1985 to start his own coffee company, Il Giornale but bought out Starbucks in 1987 and renamed it.

Under Schultz's leadership, Starbucks grew rapidly, opening new stores and expanding globally. However, the company faced challenges in the early 2000s, including increased competition, a backlash against its rapid expansion, and the 2008 global financial crisis. Schultz stepped down as CEO in 2000 but returned to the role in 2008 to help turn the company around.

Schultz is also known for his philanthropic work and advocacy for social issues. He has been a vocal supporter of veterans and has pledged to hire 10,000 of them by 2018. He has also advocated for gun control and has spoken out against President Trump's travel ban.

Schultz's story is a testament to the power of resilience and adaptability. He overcame setbacks and challenges to build one of the most successful and iconic brands in the world and has used his platform to make a positive impact on society.

The Story of Jeff Bezos

Jeff Bezos is an American entrepreneur, best known as the founder and former CEO of Amazon.com, one of the world's largest online retailers. Bezos was born in Albuquerque, New Mexico, in 1964, and was raised in Houston, Texas. He graduated from Princeton University in 1986 with degrees in electrical engineering and computer science.

After graduation, Bezos worked in the technology industry, including stints at Fitel, Bankers Trust, and D.E. Shaw & Co. In 1994, he founded Amazon.com in his garage, initially as an online bookstore. The company quickly grew and expanded into other markets, including music, movies, and electronics.

In 1997, Amazon.com went public, and Bezos became a billionaire overnight. However, the company faced a number of challenges, including the dotcom bust of the early 2000s and intense competition from other online retailers. Bezos responded by diversifying the company's offerings and investing heavily in new technology.

Under Bezos' leadership, Amazon.com became one of

the world's most successful and innovative companies, known for its customer-centric approach and cutting-edge technology. Bezos stepped down as CEO in July 2021 but remains involved with the company as its executive chairman.

Throughout his career, Bezos has demonstrated an ability to adapt to changing market conditions and capitalize on new opportunities. He has also been a strong advocate for innovation and risk-taking, encouraging his employees to "think big" and pursue bold new ideas. Bezos' success has made him one of the wealthiest people in the world, with a net worth estimated at over $100 billion.

The stories of J.K. Rowling, Walt Disney, Oprah Winfrey, Steve Jobs, Vera Wang, Jack Ma, Sheryl Sandberg, Howard Schultz, and Jeff Bezos demonstrate that career setbacks and job loss do not define your future. With resilience, perseverance, and a willingness to adapt, you can overcome any obstacle and achieve success. These individuals are shining examples of what can be achieved when you stay positive and focus on your goals, no matter how difficult the journey may be.

Chapter Seven

Overcoming Financial Hardship

From Rags to Riches

Money is a significant factor in modern society. It enables people to live comfortably and enjoy the fruits of their labor. However, financial hardship can be a massive obstacle to achieving success and happiness. It takes a certain kind of resilience to overcome poverty and achieve financial stability. In this chapter, we will explore the inspiring stories of individuals who started with very little but rose to financial prosperity through hard work, determination, and creativity.

Some of the most successful people in the world started their lives in poverty, including Oprah Winfrey and J.K. Rowling, as we saw in the previous chapter. However, many others have similar stories of overcoming financial adversity.

Chris Gardner's Story

Chris Gardner's story is one of the most inspirational rags-to-riches tales in recent history. Born in 1954 in Milwaukee, Wisconsin, he grew up in poverty and spent much of his childhood in foster care. After joining the Navy and spending some time as a medical supplies salesman, Gardner found himself homeless and jobless in San Francisco with his young son.

Despite facing numerous setbacks, Gardner remained determined to create a better life for himself and his son. He worked tirelessly to secure a spot in a highly competitive stockbroker training program, but even after being accepted, he faced immense challenges. He had no salary, no savings, and no place to live, and often had to rely on shelters and public restrooms to get by.

But Gardner refused to give up. He worked hard and persevered through the grueling training program, eventually earning a full-time job at a prestigious brokerage firm. He went on to found his own investment firm, Gardner Rich & Co., and became a multi-millionaire.

In addition to his success in the financial industry, Gardner is also known for his philanthropy and dedication to helping others overcome adversity. He has written several books, including his memoir, "The Pursuit of Happyness," which was turned into a movie starring Will Smith. He is also a motivational speaker, sharing his story of overcoming homelessness and poverty to inspire others to pursue their dreams with passion and perseverance.

Jan Koum's Story

Jan Koum is a Ukrainian-born American entrepreneur who co-founded the mobile messaging app, WhatsApp. Koum grew up in a small village in Ukraine before his family immigrated to the United States when he was 16 years old. They settled in Mountain View, California, and struggled to make ends meet.

Despite his difficult circumstances, Koum was a gifted programmer and had a passion for technology. He taught himself computer networking by reading books from a used bookstore and practicing on the computer at a local store. He eventually landed a job as an infrastructure engineer at Yahoo!, where he worked for nine years.

In 2009, Koum co-founded WhatsApp with his friend, Brian Acton. The app was designed to provide a simple and reliable way for people to communicate with each other across the world, using just their mobile phones. Initially, the app struggled to gain traction, and Koum and Acton had to rely on their savings to keep the company afloat.

However, in 2014, Facebook acquired WhatsApp for a staggering $19 billion, making Koum one of the richest people in the world. Despite his success, Koum has remained humble and focused on his mission to provide people with a secure and private way to communicate online. He has also used his wealth to give back to the community, supporting charities and organizations that help people who are less fortunate. Koum's story is a testament to the power of perseverance and the potential for success that lies within all of us, regardless of our circumstances.

Sara Blakely's Story

Sara Blakely is an American entrepreneur and businesswoman who is the founder of Spanx, a highly successful shapewear company. Born in Clearwater, Florida, Blakely faced a number of challenges early on in her life, including the divorce of her parents when she was a child and financial struggles during her early adulthood.

Despite these setbacks, Blakely remained determined to succeed. After graduating from Florida State University with a degree in communications, she began working a variety of odd jobs, including as a stand-up comedian and as a door-to-door fax machine salesperson.

It was during her time as a salesperson that Blakely had the idea for Spanx. Frustrated with the lack of comfortable and flattering undergarments for women, she decided to create her own. With $5,000 in savings, she began working on prototypes and eventually came up with a design that combined footless pantyhose with control-top underwear.

Blakely faced numerous obstacles in getting Spanx off the ground, including being turned down by numerous manufacturers and facing resistance from retailers who didn't believe that women would want to wear her product. However, she remained persistent and eventually secured a deal with Neiman Marcus to carry Spanx in its stores.

Today, Spanx is a hugely successful company, with Blakely at the helm as CEO. In addition to her work with Spanx, Blakely is also a philanthropist who supports a number of causes, including education and women's empowerment. She has been recognized for her entrepreneurship and philanthropy by numerous organizations, including the United Nations Foundation and Time magazine.

These success stories demonstrate that financial hardship does not have to be a permanent obstacle to success. With determination, hard work, and creativity, anyone can overcome poverty and achieve financial prosperity.

The Story of Ursula Burns

Ursula Burns is an American businesswoman who is best known for being the former CEO of Xerox Corporation. She was born on September 20, 1958, in New York City and grew up in a low-income housing project on the Lower East Side of Manhattan.

Burns began her career with Xerox in 1980 as a summer intern, while she was studying mechanical engineering at the Polytechnic Institute of New York University. She worked her way up the ranks, holding various positions in product development and planning, including executive assistant to the chairman and CEO.

In 2009, Burns was named the CEO of Xerox, becoming the first African American woman to lead a Fortune 500 company. She faced significant challenges during her tenure, as the company was struggling financially and had to restructure to compete in the digital age.

Under Burns' leadership, Xerox transformed from a traditional printer and copier company to a global services and technology company, expanding into areas such as IT outsourcing, cloud computing, and document management. She also oversaw Xerox's acquisition of Affiliated Computer Services, a business process outsourcing company, for $6.4 billion in 2010.

Burns retired as CEO of Xerox in 2016 and served as the chairman of Veon, a multinational telecommunications company, from 2017 to 2020. She is a board member of several companies, including ExxonMobil, Nestlé, and Uber.

Despite growing up in poverty and facing significant obstacles throughout her career, Burns rose to become one of the most successful businesswomen in the world. Her story is a testament to the power of hard work, perseverance, and determination.

Daymond John's Story

Daymond John is an entrepreneur, investor, and television personality who is best known as the founder and CEO of FUBU, a clothing company that grew from a streetwear brand into a global fashion empire. Born and raised in Queens, New York, John had a passion for fashion and entrepreneurship from a young age. He started his first business, selling handmade hats on the streets of New York City, while he was still in high school.

After high school, John attended college for a short time before dropping out to focus on his business ventures. He worked a variety of odd jobs to support himself and his budding clothing line, including working as a waiter and a security guard.

Despite facing numerous setbacks and financial struggles, John continued to pursue his dream of building a successful fashion brand. In 1992, he founded FUBU with his childhood friends, and the brand quickly gained popularity within the hip-hop community.

Over the years, John has faced many challenges in his career, including financial struggles, a failed partnership with Samsung, and even a cancer diagnosis. However, he persevered through these obstacles and continued to grow his business empire.

In addition to FUBU, John has also become a well-known investor and television personality. He is a regular on the hit show "Shark Tank," where he invests in and mentors up-and-coming entrepreneurs.

Through his success, John has become a powerful advocate for entrepreneurship and financial literacy, particularly for people from disadvantaged backgrounds. He has written several books, including "The Power of Broke," which encourages aspiring entrepreneurs to turn their financial struggles into strengths and to use their creativity and resourcefulness to build successful businesses.

Michael Bloomberg's Story

Michael Bloomberg is a billionaire businessman, philanthropist, and former mayor of New York City.

Bloomberg was born in Boston, Massachusetts, in 1942, and raised in a middle-class Jewish family. His father worked as a bookkeeper for a dairy company, and his mother was a secretary. Bloomberg attended Johns Hopkins University, where he earned a degree in electrical engineering, before attending Harvard Business School for his MBA.

After graduation, Bloomberg began his career at Salomon Brothers, a Wall Street investment bank. He quickly rose through the ranks, becoming a partner in the firm in 1972. In 1981, Bloomberg was fired from Salomon Brothers after the firm was bought by another company. With a severance package of $10 million, Bloomberg decided to start his own company, Bloomberg LP, which provides financial data and analytics to clients around the world.

Bloomberg LP started as a small start-up in a one-room office, but it quickly grew into a major player in the financial world. Today, Bloomberg LP has over 325,000 subscribers and generates over $10 billion in revenue each year. Bloomberg himself is worth over $50 billion, making him one of the richest people in the world.

In addition to his business success, Bloomberg has also been active in philanthropy and politics. He has donated billions of dollars to various causes, including public health, education, and environmental issues. He also served as the mayor of New York City for three terms, from 2002 to 2013.

Bloomberg's story is a testament to the power of hard work and determination. Despite facing setbacks in his career, he was able to use his skills and knowledge to start his own company and achieve incredible success. His dedication to giving back to his community and making a positive impact on the world is also an inspiration for others who may be facing financial hardships.

Ralph Lauren's Story

Ralph Lauren is an American fashion designer and business executive who is best known for his iconic Ralph Lauren Corporation. Lauren was born in the Bronx, New York City, in 1939 to Ashkenazi Jewish immigrant parents. Growing up, Lauren had a keen interest in fashion and style, often dreaming of becoming a millionaire by designing ties.

After dropping out of college, Lauren started working for Brooks Brothers, a high-end clothing retailer. However, he was fired after only a year and a half because the company felt that his designs were too unconventional. Lauren then went on to work for other companies but always dreamed of starting his own business.

In 1967, with a $50,000 loan, Lauren started his own company, Polo Fashions. He began by designing and selling ties under the label "Polo," which quickly became popular due to their unique and stylish designs. Lauren eventually expanded his product line to include clothing, accessories, fragrances, and even home furnishings.

Despite facing setbacks and challenges in his early career, Lauren's passion for fashion and perseverance ultimately paid off. He is one of the most successful fashion designers in the world, with a net worth of over $5 billion.

Ralph Today, Lauren is a global brand with a presence in more than 80 countries. Lauren has received numerous awards and accolades for his contributions to the fashion industry. Despite his enormous success, he remains involved in every aspect of his business and continues to innovate and push boundaries.

In addition to his fashion empire, Lauren is also known for his philanthropy and support of various charitable causes.

The Story of Richard Branson

Richard Branson is a British entrepreneur, investor, and philanthropist. He is best known for founding the Virgin Group, a conglomerate that includes more than 400 companies, ranging from airlines to media companies.

Branson was born in Surrey, England in 1950. He struggled in school due to dyslexia and dropped out at the age of 16 to start his first business, a magazine called Student. The magazine was successful, and Branson used the profits to start a mail-order record company called Virgin. The company grew quickly, and Branson opened a record store in London, which eventually led to the founding of Virgin Records.

In the 1980s, Branson expanded the Virgin brand into new industries, including airlines, with the founding of Virgin Atlantic Airways, and telecommunications, with the founding of Virgin Mobile. He has since expanded the brand to include hotels, financial services, and more.

Throughout his career, Branson has faced numerous setbacks and challenges. For example, in 1992, a fire destroyed his home on Necker Island, causing millions of dollars in damage. In 2000, a high-profile attempt to circumnavigate the globe in a hot air balloon ended in failure, and Branson nearly lost his life in the process.

Despite these setbacks, Branson has remained resilient and has continued to pursue new ventures. He is known for his adventurous spirit and willingness to take risks, such as attempting to cross the Atlantic Ocean in a speedboat and setting world records for hot air ballooning.

Branson is also a philanthropist and has used his wealth to support various causes, such as environmental conservation and fighting disease. He has pledged to donate the majority of his wealth to charity through the Giving Pledge, a commitment made by the world's wealthiest individuals to give away the majority of their wealth to address society's most pressing problems.

Overall, Branson's story is one of perseverance, innovation, and a willingness to take risks. He has faced numerous challenges throughout his career but has always bounced back and continued to push the boundaries of what is possible.

The Story of Tony Robbins

Tony Robbins is a well-known American motivational speaker, self-help author, and life coach. He is widely regarded as one of the most successful and influential figures in the personal development industry. However, his success didn't come easy, and he had to overcome many obstacles and challenges to reach where he is today.

Robbins was born in North Hollywood, California in 1960, and his childhood was not an easy one. His parents got divorced when he was only seven years old, and he had to move around a lot with his mother and siblings. As a result, he never really had a stable home life and was often subjected to physical and emotional abuse.

Despite his difficult childhood, Robbins was determined to create a better life for himself. He began reading self-help books at a young age and attended various seminars and workshops to learn more about personal development. Eventually, he became a protégé of Jim Rohn, a well-known motivational speaker, who helped him hone his skills and develop his own unique approach to personal development.

In the 1980s, Robbins began giving his own seminars and workshops, which quickly became popular among people seeking to improve their lives. He also published his first book, "Unlimited Power," which became a best-seller and cemented his position as a leading figure in the personal development industry.

Over the years, Robbins has continued to expand his empire, offering a wide range of programs, courses, and products designed to help people achieve their goals and overcome their fears and limitations. He has worked with many high-profile clients, including Oprah Winfrey, Serena Williams, and Bill Clinton, and has become a household name around the world.

Despite his success, Robbins has faced some criticism

over the years, particularly for his controversial methods and some of the claims he has made. However, he remains one of the most influential and successful figures in the personal development industry, inspiring millions of people around the world to achieve their full potential and live their best lives.

These success stories demonstrate that financial hardship does not have to be a permanent obstacle to success. With determination, hard work, and creativity, anyone can overcome poverty and achieve financial prosperity.

Chapter Eight

Standing Up to Injustice

Overcoming Discrimination and Prejudice

Discrimination and prejudice have plagued societies around the world for centuries, often leading to acts of violence and oppression against marginalized groups. However, there have also been countless individuals who have stood up to injustice, advocating for their rights and those of others, and paving the way for a more equitable future.

In this chapter, we will explore the experiences of individuals from various backgrounds who have faced discrimination and prejudice, and how they overcame these challenges to achieve success and make a difference in the world. Their stories serve as a reminder that, even in the face of adversity, we have the power to create positive change and make a difference.

The leading example is that of Mahatma Gandhi: Gandhi was an Indian activist who fought for India's independence from British rule. He faced discrimination and prejudice as an Indian living under British colonial rule, and he worked tirelessly to change the oppressive laws and policies that kept his people down. His nonviolent methods inspired movements for civil rights and freedom around the world.

Another inspiring story is that of Nelson Mandela, the former President of South Africa who fought tirelessly against apartheid, a system of institutionalized racial segregation and discrimination.

In the United States, civil rights activist Rosa Parks is remembered for her role in the Montgomery Bus Boycott, a protest against racial segregation on public transportation.

Cesar Chavez was a Mexican American labor leader and civil rights activist who fought for the rights of migrant workers in the United States. We feature his story here.

Another story is of Temple Grandin, an American author, professor, and activist. Diagnosed with autism at a young age and faced discrimination and prejudice from a society that did not understand her condition. She went on to become a leading expert on animal behavior and an advocate for the rights of people with autism, helping to change the way society views and treats people with disabilities.

Misty Copeland is an American ballet dancer and the first African-American woman to be promoted to principal dancer at the American Ballet Theatre. We feature his story here.

The story of Harvey Milk, the first openly gay elected

official in California, is another example of standing up to discrimination and prejudice.

Another story we feature is that of James Baldwin, an African American writer, and social critic who lived during the Civil Rights Movement. Baldwin faced discrimination and prejudice throughout his life, but he used his writing to challenge societal norms and advocate for equality.

We also feature the story of Ellen DeGeneres, a comedian and television host who came out as a lesbian on her show in 1997. At the time, it was a bold move that could have jeopardized her career, but Ellen stood up for her identity and has since become an icon in the LGBTQ+ community.

These stories are just a few examples of the many people who have overcome discrimination and prejudice through their unwavering determination and resilience.

The Story of Mahatma Gandhi

Mohandas Karamchand Gandhi, better known as Mahatma Gandhi, was an Indian political and spiritual leader who is known for his nonviolent philosophy of civil disobedience. He was born in 1869 in Porbandar, India, and was the youngest of three sons. He studied law in London and then went to South Africa to work as a lawyer, where he first became involved in activism against the discrimination of the Indian community.

In 1915, Gandhi returned to India and began to lead the Indian National Congress in the struggle for independence from British colonial rule. He advocated for nonviolent resistance, civil disobedience, and peaceful protest as a means of achieving political and social change. He also worked to improve the conditions of the untouchables, a marginalized and oppressed group in India's caste system.

Throughout his life, Gandhi faced opposition and violence from the British colonial government who disagreed with his methods. He was imprisoned several times. Despite these challenges, Gandhi remained committed to his principles of nonviolence and was eventually successful in leading India to independence in 1947.

Gandhi's legacy has had a lasting impact on the world, inspiring civil rights movements and activists around the globe. His teachings on nonviolence, peaceful resistance, and social justice continue to influence movements for change and inspire those fighting against discrimination and oppression.

Nelson Mandela's Story

Nelson Mandela was a South African anti-apartheid revolutionary, politician, and philanthropist who served as the President of South Africa from 1994 to 1999. Born on July 18, 1918, in Mvezo, a small village in the Eastern Cape province of South Africa, he was the son of a Thembu chief. Mandela was given the name "Rolihlahla," which means "troublemaker," by his father.

Mandela was educated at the University of Fort Hare

and the University of Witwatersrand, where he studied law. He became involved in politics in 1944 when he joined the African National Congress (ANC), a political party that aimed to end the system of apartheid in South Africa. Apartheid was a system of racial segregation that was imposed by the white minority government of South Africa in 1948, and it denied black South Africans basic human rights, such as the right to vote, to own property, or to live where they chose.

In 1952, Mandela became one of the leaders of the ANC's campaign against apartheid. He advocated for non-violent resistance at first, but after the Sharpeville massacre in 1960, where police killed 69 unarmed protesters, Mandela believed that peaceful protest was no longer effective. He co-founded the ANC's armed wing, Umkhonto we Sizwe, which waged a guerrilla war against the government.

In 1962, Mandela was arrested and sentenced to life imprisonment for sabotage and conspiracy to overthrow the government. He was sent to Robben Island, a notorious prison off the coast of Cape Town, where he spent 27 years in a tiny cell. Despite his imprisonment, Mandela became an international symbol of resistance to apartheid.

In 1990, after mounting pressure from the international community, the South African government released Mandela from prison. He emerged as a national hero and continued to work toward the end of apartheid. In 1994, South Africa held its first democratic elections, and Mandela became the country's first black president. He used his presidency to work toward national reconciliation and to address the deep-seated racial tensions that apartheid had left behind. He stepped down as president in 1999 but continued to work for social justice and human rights until his death in 2013.

Mandela's life and legacy are a testament to the power of resilience and perseverance in the face of injustice. He fought against a system that sought to deny him and his people their basic human rights, and he did so with a determination that inspired millions around the world. His commitment to non-violence, even in the face of brutality and oppression, serves as a model for social and political activism to this day. Mandela remains an icon of the struggle for racial equality and human dignity, and his legacy will continue to inspire future generations to fight against injustice and inequality.

The Story of Rosa Parks

Rosa Parks was an American civil rights activist who played a crucial role in the Montgomery Bus Boycott, which began in 1955. At the time, segregation was still widespread in the United States, and one of the most visible symbols of this discrimination was the separate seating arrangements for whites and blacks on public transportation. In Montgomery, Alabama, the law required that African Americans give up their seats to white passengers if the "white section" of the bus was full. They were also required to enter through the back door of the bus.

On December 1, 1955, Parks boarded a bus in Montgomery and took a seat in the "colored section." As the bus filled up and more white passengers boarded, the driver demanded that Parks and three other African Americans give up their seats to make room. The other three eventually complied, but Parks refused. She was arrested and charged with violating Montgomery's segregation laws.

Parks' arrest sparked outrage in Montgomery's black community, and local leaders, including Martin Luther King Jr., organized a boycott of Montgomery's buses. The boycott lasted for over a year, during which time black residents carpooled or walked to work instead of using the buses. The boycott received national attention and led to the eventual desegregation of Montgomery's buses.

Parks' act of defiance made her a symbol of the civil rights movement and inspired others to stand up against racial discrimination. She continued to work as an activist throughout her life, fighting for voting rights, desegregation, and other civil rights issues. Parks passed away in 2005 at the age of 92, but her legacy as a civil rights icon lives on.

Cesar Chavez's Story

Cesar Chavez was a civil rights activist who dedicated his life to the betterment of farm workers in America. He was born in Arizona in 1927 and grew up in a family of migrant farm workers. Throughout his youth, Chavez saw firsthand the struggles of the working poor and experienced discrimination against Mexican Americans. After serving in the Navy during World War II, Chavez became a community organizer and began advocating for the rights of farm workers.

In the early 1960s, Chavez co-founded the National Farm Workers Association, which later became the United Farm Workers (UFW) union. The UFW aimed to improve the working conditions of farm laborers, many of whom were Mexican Americans, by fighting for better wages, access to healthcare, and improved working conditions. Chavez led the union in a series of strikes and boycotts, which ultimately led to increased recognition and protection of workers' rights.

One of the most notable campaigns that Chavez led was the Delano grape strike in California in 1965. The strike began when Filipino farm workers, who were members of the Agricultural Workers Organizing Committee, walked off the job demanding better pay and working conditions. Chavez's union joined the strike, and it soon grew into a nationwide boycott of grapes. The boycott lasted five years and brought national attention to the plight of farm workers. Eventually, growers agreed to recognize the UFW and sign contracts that improved workers' wages and working conditions.

Chavez continued to fight for farm workers' rights until his death in 1993. He was a tireless advocate for social justice and inspired a generation of activists to fight for workers' rights and social equality. His legacy lives on through the continued efforts of organizations dedicated to improving the lives of farm workers and other marginalized groups in America.

The Story of Temple Grandin

Temple Grandin is an American scientist, inventor, and author who revolutionized the livestock industry with her humane animal handling systems. She was born in Boston, Massachusetts in 1947, and was diagnosed with autism at the age of two.

Despite facing challenges in social interaction and communication, Grandin excelled academically and earned a bachelor's degree in psychology from Franklin Pierce College and a master's degree in animal science from Arizona State University. She later went on to earn a Ph.D. in animal science from the University of Illinois at Urbana-Champaign.

Grandin's innovative ideas about animal welfare were inspired by her autism, as she has a unique way of visualizing the world. She designed a more humane cattle-handling system that reduces stress on the animals, making it more efficient and less harmful for them. Her system involves the use of curved chutes and solid walls that prevent cattle from seeing people and objects that may cause them to panic.

Grandin has authored several books, including "Thinking in Pictures," which describes how her unique visual thinking has helped her understand the behavior of animals. She has also been recognized for her contributions to the livestock industry and her advocacy for animal welfare. In 2010, she was named one of Time magazine's 100 most influential people in the world.

Despite facing discrimination and skepticism from

those who doubted her abilities due to her autism, Grandin persevered and changed the way the world thinks about animal welfare. Her story serves as an inspiration to those who face similar challenges and encourages society to embrace diversity and the unique perspectives of individuals with autism.

Misty Copeland's Story

Misty Copeland is an American ballet dancer who has faced numerous obstacles in her career but has overcome them to become one of the most successful and influential dancers of her generation. Copeland was born in Kansas City, Missouri, in 1982, and was raised in a single-parent household. Her mother struggled with financial difficulties and was unable to afford dance lessons, so Copeland didn't start ballet until she was 13 years old.

Despite starting late, Copeland quickly showed promise as a dancer and was soon performing with a local dance company. However, she faced discrimination because of her race and body type, which didn't fit the traditional mold of a ballet dancer. Despite this, Copeland persevered and continued to work hard, eventually joining the American Ballet Theatre (ABT) as a member of the corps de Ballet.

In 2007, Copeland became the first African American female soloist in ABT's history, a major achievement in a field that has historically been dominated by white dancers. Since then, she has become a principal dancer with the company, one of the highest honors in the ballet world. Copeland has also used her platform to advocate for diversity and inclusion in dance and has become a role model for young dancers around the world.

In addition to her work with ABT, Copeland has also written several books, including her memoir "Life in Motion: An Unlikely Ballerina," which details her struggles with racism and body image issues throughout her career. She has also been the subject of several documentaries, including the 2015 film "A Ballerina's Tale," which chronicles her rise to stardom in the ballet world. Overall, Copeland's story is one of perseverance and dedication in the face of discrimination and adversity, and she continues to inspire others to follow their dreams and overcome obstacles to achieve their goals.

Harvey Milk's Story

Harvey Milk was a trailblazing American politician and activist who became the first openly gay person elected to public office in California. Milk was born in 1930 in Woodmere, New York, and grew up on Long Island. He served in the U.S. Navy during the Korean War and later worked as a Wall Street financial analyst before moving to San Francisco in 1972.

In San Francisco, Milk opened a camera store in the Castro District, a predominantly gay neighborhood, and became increasingly involved in local politics and activism. He ran unsuccessfully for the San Francisco Board of Supervisors in 1973 and 1975, but his campaigns helped to galvanize the city's LGBTQ+ community and establish him as a prominent figure in the movement.

In 1977, Milk launched a third campaign for the Board of Supervisors, and this time he won, becoming the first openly gay person elected to public office in California. As a supervisor, Milk championed a range of progressive causes, including affordable housing, police reform, and LGBTQ+ rights. He also helped to defeat a ballot initiative that would have banned gay people from teaching in California's public schools.

Milk's time in office was tragically short-lived. In November 1978, he and San Francisco Mayor George Moscone were assassinated by Dan White, a former supervisor who had resigned but wanted his job back. The murders stunned the city and the LGBTQ+ community, and thousands of people took to the streets to mourn Milk's passing and protest against anti-gay violence and discrimination.

Despite his brief time in office, Milk's legacy as a pioneering LGBTQ+ activist and politician endures to this day. His life and death inspired a generation of activists to continue the fight for LGBTQ+ rights, and his story has been the subject of numerous books, films, and documentaries. In 2009, Milk was posthumously awarded the Presidential Medal of Freedom by President Barack Obama.

The Story of James Baldwin

James Baldwin was an American novelist, essayist, and playwright, who was born on August 2, 1924, in Harlem, New York City. He was the oldest of nine children and grew up in poverty. Baldwin's stepfather, who was a preacher, was abusive, and Baldwin turned to writing as a way to escape his difficult home life.

Baldwin's writing focused on issues of race, sexuality, and class. He gained recognition in the 1950s and 1960s as a major literary figure during the civil rights movement. His works, which included novels, plays, and essays, often explored the experiences of Black Americans in the United States.

Baldwin's best-known works include "Go Tell It on the Mountain," a semi-autobiographical novel about growing up in Harlem, and "The Fire Next Time," a collection of essays that addressed issues of racism and discrimination. Baldwin was also a prominent voice in the LGBT community and wrote about his own experiences as a gay man in his later works.

Throughout his life, Baldwin was an activist and participated in various civil rights protests and marches, including the March on Washington in 1963. He also worked closely with other prominent figures in the civil rights movement, including Martin Luther King Jr. and Malcolm X.

Baldwin's writing and activism were groundbreaking, and he played a significant role in shaping the civil rights movement and promoting social justice in the United States. He died on December 1, 1987, at the age of 63, leaving behind a legacy of powerful, thought-provoking works that continue to inspire and educate readers today.

Ellen DeGeneres's Story

Ellen DeGeneres is an American comedian, actress, writer, producer, and talk show host who has become one of the most beloved figures in American entertainment. She was born on January 26, 1958, in Metairie, Louisiana, and grew up in a Christian Scientist family. Her parents divorced when she was a teenager, and her mother remarried a salesman named Roy Gruessendorf, who would later adopt Ellen.

Ellen began performing stand-up comedy in the early 1980s, and her unique style of observational humor quickly won her a following. In 1986, she appeared on "The Tonight Show Starring Johnny Carson" and became the first female comedian to be invited to sit on the show's couch after her performance.

In 1994, Ellen starred in her own sitcom, "Ellen," which became a cultural phenomenon. The show was groundbreaking for its portrayal of a gay lead character, and Ellen used the show's platform to come out as a lesbian in a highly publicized episode in 1997. While the episode was praised by many, it also led to a backlash, with some viewers and advertisers boycotting the show. Despite the controversy, Ellen continued to advocate for LGBTQ+ rights and became an icon in the community.

After "Ellen" ended in 1998, Ellen's career hit a rough patch. She struggled to find work, and her reputation suffered as rumors circulated about her being difficult to work with. But Ellen persevered and eventually landed her own daytime talk show, "The Ellen DeGeneres Show," which premiered in 2003. The show quickly became a hit, with Ellen's affable personality, comedic timing, and charitable acts winning over audiences.

Throughout her career, Ellen has been an advocate for various social causes, including animal rights, environmentalism, and LGBTQ+ rights. She has also used her platform to promote kindness and positivity, with her catchphrase "Be kind to one another" becoming a rallying cry for her fans.

Despite the success and adoration, Ellen has faced her fair share of controversies, including allegations of fostering a toxic work environment on her show. However, she has also taken responsibility for these issues and vowed to make changes to ensure a better workplace culture.

Overall, Ellen DeGeneres's story is one of perseverance, resilience, and using one's platform for good. She has overcome adversity and remained true to herself, inspiring millions along the way.

Chapter Nine

When Disaster Strikes

Overcoming Natural Disasters and Catastrophes

Natural disasters and catastrophes can strike without warning and leave behind a trail of destruction and despair. From earthquakes and hurricanes to tsunamis and wildfires, these events can be devastating and life-altering for those who are affected. In such situations, it can be easy to lose hope and succumb to the overwhelming challenges that come with rebuilding homes, communities, and lives. However, in the face of disaster, there are countless stories of resilience and triumph where individuals and communities have come together to overcome adversity and rebuild stronger than ever. These stories serve as powerful examples of human strength, perseverance, and hope in the face of unimaginable devastation.

One such story is from the time when Hurricane Katrina struck the Gulf Coast of the United States in 2005. The storm, which was one of the deadliest and most destructive hurricanes in U.S. history, left thousands dead and caused billions of dollars in damage. In the aftermath of the hurricane, many people were displaced from their homes and left struggling to rebuild their lives.

One of those trying times, an inspiring example is the story of Brad Pitt and his organization, Make It Right. Pitt was moved by the devastation he witnessed in the Lower Ninth Ward of New Orleans, one of the hardest-hit areas, and he set out to make a difference. His story is narrated in this chapter.

Another example is the story of the people of Sendai, Japan, who were struck by a devastating earthquake and tsunami in 2011. Despite the overwhelming destruction, the people of Sendai came together to help each other rebuild. The city's mayor, Emiko Okuyama, became a symbol of resilience and hope as she worked tirelessly to lead the recovery efforts and inspire her community to keep moving forward.

In addition to these examples, there are countless stories of individuals who have overcome natural disasters and catastrophes. These stories remind us that even in the darkest of times, there is hope, and that together, we can overcome even the greatest of challenges.

One such individual is Amanda Lindhout, a Canadian journalist who was kidnapped and held captive for 460 days in Somalia. Lindhout was in the country to cover the ongoing conflict and was abducted along with her colleague. During her captivity, Lindhout was subjected to horrific conditions and abuse, but she refused to give up hope. Instead, she drew on her inner strength and resilience to survive. Her story follows.

We tell the story of Aron Ralston, a hiker who was trapped in a remote canyon in Utah for five days and was forced to amputate his own arm to free himself but went on to become a motivational speaker and author.

We follow with the story of Antoinette Tuff, a bookkeeper who prevented a mass shooting at an elementary school in Atlanta by talking to the gunman and convincing him to surrender.

We also tell the story of Aaron Feuerstein, the CEO of Malden Mills, a textile factory in Massachusetts that was destroyed by a fire, but he chose to keep paying his employees and rebuild the factory, even though it put the company under financial strain.

We follow the above story with that of Kiki Katese, a Rwandan woman who founded the first female drumming troupe in Rwanda after the country's devastating genocide, providing healing and empowerment for the women who had suffered through the tragedy.

We conclude with the story of Malvika Iyer, a bomb blast survivor who lost both her hands and suffered severe injuries to her legs but went on to become a disability rights activist, motivational speaker, and social worker.

These stories remind us that even in the face of disaster, there is always hope. They show us that when we come together and support one another, we can overcome even the greatest of challenges.

Brad Pitt and His Organization Make It Right's Story

Brad Pitt is a well-known Hollywood actor who is also renowned for his philanthropic efforts. In 2005, when Hurricane Katrina devastated the city of New Orleans, Brad Pitt was among the many people who were horrified by the destruction and the suffering caused by the natural disaster.

Determined to help the people of New Orleans, Brad Pitt founded the Make It Right Foundation in 2007. The aim of the organization was to help rebuild homes in the city's Lower Ninth Ward, one of the areas that was hardest hit by Hurricane Katrina.

Pitt was not content with just providing basic housing. Instead, he wanted to create homes that were environmentally sustainable, affordable, and aesthetically pleasing. He assembled a team of architects and designers to create innovative and eco-friendly designs for the homes.

Despite facing numerous challenges along the way, including resistance from local officials and the difficulty of finding suitable land to build on, Pitt and his team remained dedicated to the cause. They eventually managed to build 109 homes in the Lower Ninth Ward, providing a safe and comfortable place for residents to live.

Make It Right has not only helped to rebuild homes in the Lower Ninth Ward but has also provided jobs and training opportunities for local residents, helping to boost the local economy. Brad Pitt's efforts have also helped to raise awareness about the ongoing struggles faced by the people of New Orleans in the aftermath of Hurricane Katrina.

Through his work with Make It Right, Brad Pitt has demonstrated how one person's determination and compassion can make a significant difference in the lives of many. He has shown that even in the face of disaster, there is always hope and the possibility of creating positive change.

The Story of Mayor Emiko Okuyama of Sendai, Japan

Mayor Emiko Okuyama became the face of resilience during the 2011 earthquake and tsunami that hit Sendai, Japan. The disaster was a 9.0 magnitude earthquake that triggered a massive tsunami, killing over 15,000 people and leaving many more injured and homeless. Mayor Okuyama played a key role in leading the city's response and recovery efforts.

Despite being in a city that was completely devastated by the disaster, Mayor Okuyama remained calm and composed. She quickly organized the evacuation of citizens to higher ground, set up emergency shelters, and worked tirelessly to coordinate rescue and recovery efforts. She also ensured that accurate information was disseminated to the public, which helped to prevent panic and chaos.

In the aftermath of the disaster, Mayor Okuyama led the efforts to rebuild the city, which included building new infrastructure, providing psychological support to those affected by the disaster, and finding ways to restore the city's economy. Her leadership and resilience were instrumental in the city's recovery and helped to inspire hope in the midst of a tragic event.

Mayor Okuyama's story is a testament to the power of leadership and resilience in the face of disaster. Despite the enormity of the challenge she faced, she remained committed to her community and worked tirelessly to ensure that they were able to recover and rebuild. Her story is an inspiration to all those who face adversity and serves as a reminder that we can overcome even the most difficult of challenges if we remain resilient and committed to our goals.

Amanda Lindhout's Story

Amanda Lindhout is a Canadian journalist and humanitarian who survived 460 days in captivity in Somalia. Born in 1981 in Alberta, Canada, Amanda was passionate about travel from a young age. She worked multiple jobs to save money for travel and eventually became a successful freelance journalist. In 2008, she traveled to Somalia to report on the civil war and humanitarian crisis in the country.

On August 23, 2008, Amanda was kidnapped along with her Australian colleague Nigel Brennan and held for ransom by a group of gunmen. They were kept in captivity for over a year in extremely harsh conditions, and subjected to torture, starvation, and abuse. Despite the difficult circumstances, Amanda remained determined to survive and maintain her mental and emotional strength. She taught herself meditation and learned to find small joys in her surroundings, such as watching ants or counting the number of steps she took each day.

Throughout her captivity, Amanda's family and friends worked tirelessly to negotiate her release and raise the ransom money. Finally, after 15 months in captivity, Amanda and Nigel were released in November 2009 after their families paid a large ransom.

After her release, Amanda returned to Canada and began the process of rebuilding her life. She founded the Global Enrichment Foundation, a nonprofit organization that provides education and community development programs in Somalia and has become a prominent public speaker and advocate for human rights and peacebuilding. Amanda's resilience and strength in the face of extreme adversity serve as an inspiration to many, and her story has been shared in numerous media outlets and in her memoir, "A House in the Sky".

The Story of Aron Ralston

Aron Ralston is an American mountaineer, engineer, and motivational speaker who gained international attention in 2003 when he became trapped by a boulder in an isolated slot canyon in Utah, USA. While canyoneering alone, Ralston's right forearm became pinned beneath a boulder for nearly five days. With no way to call for help, he was forced to use a dull multi-tool knife to amputate his own arm in order to free himself and seek medical attention.

Ralston was an experienced climber and had successfully completed many challenging climbs before his accident. However, on this particular day, he didn't tell anyone where he was going and did not bring adequate supplies or equipment, such as a rope or a satellite phone, which would have allowed him to call for help.

After his accident, Ralston was able to rappel down a 65-foot cliff and hike out of the canyon, where he was eventually found and rescued by a family who happened to be hiking in the area. He was flown to a hospital in Grand Junction, Colorado, where he underwent surgery to treat the amputation.

Despite the traumatic experience, Ralston remained resilient and went on to continue his mountaineering career. He also wrote a memoir about his experience, called "Between a Rock and a Hard Place," which was later adapted into the Academy Award-nominated film "127 Hours," starring James Franco as Ralston.

Through his experience, Ralston learned the importance of being prepared, communicating with loved ones, and appreciating life. He has since become an advocate for outdoor safety and speaks publicly about his experience, encouraging others to take safety precautions and avoid making the same mistakes he did.

Antoinette Tuff's Story

Antoinette Tuff is a remarkable woman who displayed incredible courage and compassion in the face of danger.

On August 20, 2013, Tuff was working as a bookkeeper at the Ronald E. McNair Discovery Learning Academy in Decatur, Georgia, when a 20-year-old man named Michael Hill entered the school armed with an AK-47 assault rifle and 500 rounds of ammunition.

Hill began shooting at the school, and Tuff found herself face-to-face with the gunman. She quickly realized that she was the only person who could stop him and prevent a tragedy from unfolding. Tuff remained calm and began talking to Hill, using her own life experiences to connect with him and build a rapport.

Tuff spent the next hour and a half on the phone with 911, relaying Hill's demands and keeping him calm. She talked to him about her own struggles, including a suicide attempt, and helped him to see that there was a way out of his situation that did not involve violence. Tuff was able to convince Hill to put down his weapon and surrender to the police.

Thanks to Tuff's bravery and quick thinking, no one was hurt in the incident. Tuff received numerous accolades for her heroism, including being named one of CNN's Heroes of the Year in 2013. She has since become an advocate for mental health and gun control, using her own experience to help others who may be struggling with similar issues. Tuff's story is a powerful reminder that one person can make a difference, even in the face of overwhelming adversity.

The Story of Aaron Feuerstein

Aaron Feuerstein, a businessman, and owner of Malden Mills, a textile factory in Lawrence, Massachusetts, faced a crisis in 1995 when the factory burned down. The fire destroyed nearly one-third of the factory and left over 3,000 employees jobless just before the holiday season. Instead of abandoning the factory and moving the business to a cheaper location, Feuerstein decided to rebuild the factory and continue operations in Lawrence.

Feuerstein was known for his commitment to his employees, and despite the financial burden of rebuilding the factory, he made the decision to continue paying the employees' salaries and benefits during the reconstruction process. This decision was especially significant, as the textile industry was facing significant pressure from overseas competition, and many believed that the future of the industry in the United States was bleak.

Feuerstein's actions were not only financially risky, but they were also a testament to his values and beliefs. He believed that the company had a responsibility to its employees and the community, and he refused to compromise on that responsibility even in the face of such adversity. He stated, "Business is about more than making a profit. It's about making a difference in people's lives."

Despite the challenges and criticisms he faced, Feuerstein's decision to rebuild the factory and support his employees paid off. Malden Mills became the first textile factory in the world to be fully rebuilt after a fire, and Feuerstein's commitment to his employees helped to inspire loyalty and dedication from his workforce. The company continued to operate successfully until Feuerstein's retirement in 2007.

Feuerstein's story is an inspiring example of how standing up for one's values and principles can lead to success in business, even in the face of adversity. His actions remind us that businesses have the power to make a positive impact on their employees and communities and that sometimes, doing the right thing can also be the best thing for the bottom line.

Kiki Katese's Story

Kiki Katese is a Rwandan woman who used her love for the arts to bring healing and empowerment to women who had suffered greatly during the Rwandan Genocide. Kiki was born in 1974 in the southern province of Rwanda, where she grew up as the youngest of eight children. She was an artist and playwright, who had studied at the National University of Rwanda.

In 2004, Kiki founded the Rwanda Women's Interests Network (RWIN), a group that aimed to bring women together to heal and rebuild their lives after the genocide. Kiki believed that the arts could be used to help women overcome trauma, so she began to teach them how to create beautiful handicrafts, such as baskets, textiles, and pottery.

Kiki started with a group of just 20 women, but as word spread about her program, more and more women joined. Soon, there were over 200 women participating in the program. Kiki worked tirelessly to help these women not only create beautiful art but also to help them build their confidence and self-esteem.

One of Kiki's most significant achievements was the founding of the Ingoma Nshya, a women's drumming troupe. In Rwandan culture, drumming is traditionally a male-dominated activity, but Kiki believed that women should have the opportunity to participate as well. The troupe was made up of 60 women who had been affected by the genocide, and it quickly became a symbol of hope and resilience in the community.

Kiki's work has received international recognition, and she has won numerous awards for her efforts. In 2010, she was invited to attend the TEDGlobal conference in Tanzania, where she gave a powerful talk about her work with the women of Rwanda. Her story has inspired many people around the world to use the arts as a tool for healing and empowerment.

Through her work with RWIN and the Ingoma Nshya, Kiki Katese has shown that even in the aftermath of a tragedy as devastating as the Rwandan Genocide, there is still hope for healing and rebuilding. Her story is a testament to the power of art, community, and the human spirit.

The Story of Malvika Iyer

Malvika Iyer is a motivational speaker, disability rights activist, and a bomb blast survivor from India. At the age of 13, Malvika suffered a bomb blast accident at her home which resulted in the loss of both her hands and severe injuries to her legs. The incident left her shattered, and she spent months in the hospital undergoing surgeries and treatments. However, with the support of her family and a strong will to overcome her disability, Malvika went on to achieve incredible success.

Malvika completed her higher education, obtained a Ph.D. in social work, and started working as a disability rights activist, advocating for the rights of people with disabilities. She has been invited to speak at various national and international platforms, including the United Nations, TEDx, and the Women's Economic Forum, where she has shared her story of resilience and motivated others to overcome their challenges.

Malvika has also been recognized with several awards for her contributions to the field of disability rights and advocacy, including the Women Transforming India Award, the NCPEDP-Mindtree Helen Keller Award, and the prestigious Forbes 30 Under 30 Asia Award.

Malvika's story is a testament to the power of resilience, determination, and perseverance. Despite facing incredible adversity, she refused to let her disability define her and went on to become a voice for others with disabilities, inspiring and empowering them to live a life of dignity and purpose.

Conclusion

The Resilient Spirit

Throughout this book, we have seen the incredible stories of individuals who have faced adversities in various forms from discrimination and prejudice to natural disasters and personal tragedies. These individuals did not let their circumstances define them; instead, they found the strength within themselves to overcome their challenges and emerge stronger than ever before.

Their stories serve as a reminder of the power of the human spirit and the resilience that lies within each and every one of us. We all face difficulties in our lives, but it is how we respond to them that truly matters.

As we reflect on these stories, we are reminded that resilience is not something that can be taught or acquired overnight. It is a lifelong journey that requires courage, perseverance, and a willingness to embrace change.

Despite the challenges they faced, the individuals in this book refused to give up. They found creative solutions, sought out support from their communities, and never lost sight of their goals. They showed us that, even in the darkest of times, there is always hope.

Their stories also highlight the importance of empathy and compassion. Many of these individuals found the strength to overcome their challenges through the kindness and support of others. By showing empathy and understanding to those around us, we can create a more resilient and supportive community for all.

In conclusion, the resilient spirit is within all of us. We must embrace our challenges, seek out support, and never give up on our dreams. Let us draw inspiration from the stories in this book and strive to live our lives with courage, determination, and compassion.

About the Author

Pranav Pandya, the accomplished Information Technology professional behind this inspiring self-help book has had a remarkable career spanning four decades. With enriching experiences in India, the Middle East, the USA, and Europe, he has established himself as a business development expert with a deep understanding of global markets.

Throughout his career, he has been driven by a passion for learning and growth. But in recent years, he has embarked on a deliberate journey to prioritize his other passions: photography, traveling, music, and writing. He currently resides in Mumbai, where he draws inspiration from the city's vibrant culture and rich history.

In this captivating book, the author shares his profound insights and wisdom, garnered from a lifetime of personal and professional experiences, to empower readers on their path to unlocking their fullest potential. His commitment to uplifting others is evident on every page of this book, which is both insightful and inspiring.

Despite his many accomplishments, the author remains an avid learner, always eager to keep pace with the latest news and developments. He maintains a particular fascination with cutting-edge technologies, especially in the realm of InfoTech, with a strong focus on artificial intelligence and cyber security.

Enriched by a fulfilling family life as a devoted husband and father, the author's multifaceted experiences have profoundly influenced his distinctive outlook on attaining success and fulfillment in our contemporary, fast-paced world. With a firm belief in the untapped potential within each individual, the author's book offers invaluable tools and a wellspring of inspiration to empower readers to transform their aspirations into tangible reality.

Join the author on a transformative journey as he inspires and equips you with the tools to reach new heights in your personal and professional endeavors. This captivating blend of wisdom, passion, and expertise is a testament to his unwavering commitment to making a positive impact on the lives of others.

www.ingramcontent.com/pod-product-compliance
Lightning Source LLC
LaVergne TN
LVHW050318160826
845677LV00014B/3468

* 9 7 8 8 1 9 6 0 8 9 5 6 6 *